In the afterMATH of WuHan
Certain things that still didn't ADD up as the
cold bodies continued to pile up.

ISBN

Fonts by Jess Latham. Thank You.

Printed, Distributed and Bound in the United States of America First Printing

June 2020

Published by He Who Rebels Against All

Oklahoma City, Oklahoma 73106

Hey, Thanks for getting a copy!

Facebook.com/TylerLazarus1992

Facebook.com/Odditlyer

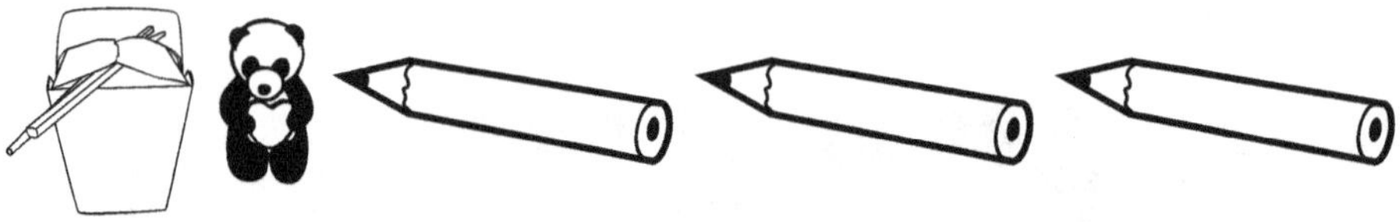

1+1+1+1+1+2+3+89,149+73,471+190,329+1+1+1+1
+22,549

In the afterMATH of Wuhan:
Certain things that still didn't ADD up as the cold bodies continued to pile up.

This is the follow up.
I'm not going to play follow the leader,
when I am THE leader.

Preface/Gameface:

catching breath

This is my third book release in ONE year, bitch-jes. I'm not writing this to sound badass or to impress anyone (like anyone really cares what authors are up to LMAO) but I need to explain #SOME-TING.

In the old days, writers would write one book and then go off and have a mental breakdown somewhere.

Author Biographical studies of what they were doing when not writing is hilariously lame.

LONG GONE are the days of creating a product, and going off to cry and get fat ????? for a few years because of the mental exertion required, which I guess was too much.

There is NO reason a writer cannot be in constant contact with the market,
without over-saturating it, and being able to pump out new material on a less

dramatic time table of decades lmao...

There is no relaxatioN!!! *TASKMASTER 3000 FIRES UP*

I get it, nothing is very natural about sitting in a cramped space hammering out ideas for 14 hours a day.

That isn't healthy lmao, but writing is what it is.

As their writing quality improves, their mental state DECLINES, sharply.

Cognitive space becomes replaced by heavy emotions, and then they SUI out.

Ok, like, I dont have time for all that.

I wanna distance myself from other 'artiste-s.'
While writing IS an art form, I'd rather not have the title of ARTIST, hovering above #ME because it's completely meaningless. I know what I am.

I watch these other "artists" trying their whole career to receive the starry crown of ARTISTE!!!!!
Begging the public to validate them with some unspoken ceremonial acceptance.

The Desperation.
Bitch, Please.

I'm here to take away ALL the nonsense from writing.
The neurosis. The Psychosis. The Fluff.
Were not cutting our ear off, and throwing paint on a wall.
Once again, please dont lump me in with those mental patients with paintbrushes.

If you're writing about your feelings, you're journaling.
You aint WRITING nothing but shit we all go through.
By all means, if you need that to declutter ya mind, honey, go ahead and Pop Ya Percocet.
But ya Boring ass wanna-be memoir is not the same as a written piece of Lit-tuh-chur.

Nobody currr about the boy or girl who broke your heart
and sent you spiraling down into alcoholism

It's about self-discipline, hardwork, and an imperial work ethic, more than some self-absorbed paint splatter ruining the furniture and the floor.

BYEEEEEE

Give me the towel, I'm goin in, hoe

I am the Nicki Minaj of the Literary World

makes faces into the camera

sticks tongue out at the critics

WOOH LORD
In the afterMATH of Wuhan,
The things that still didn't ADD up
as the cold bodies continued to pile.

a final word, deleted scene of KONG FLU PANDA

The supervisor of the Chinese national health
commission - LIU DENGFENG - goes on record
admitting (confirming at the highest level)
that the Chinese government issued an executive order
to dispose of Corona virus vials.

"To prevent secondary disasters"
But not a coverup, he insists
LIU goes on to say that specific labs
were unauthorized to handle those pathogen samples
and not able to meet the requirements to be handling them

From China. In a lab. Inside one specific lab,
not supposed to be touching them.

Wonder WHICH lab that it could possibly be???
????

Hmm.. gee golly!~ better play devil's advocate here

and deny the truth~~~~ again.

stares at the silent jury *furious*

judge loudly bangs the gavel

Guilty. Of all charges.
YA MOTHAFUCKIN, RIGHT!

Chapter I.

We've got a confession, an admission of lab neglect,
a trail of paper leading back to the lab notes, themselves.

It's been conclusively ascertained that this is where it came from.

HELL, the CHINESE CDC just admitted that COVID .... did not... come...
from.... teh... WHET.... MAR-KITT.

Lmao. Okay. Told U so times One Million and Fifty Five Thousand.

But as was said in the previous novel, it wont be able to take back the death count thats already happened.

But it IS important to finally have a conclusive origin story, instead of smoke, mirrors and denial.

Knowing where it started can't reverse the loss of life,
but it does set things in the books, of how, when, why, and

WHO.

It all sounds incredibly insulated from an outside perspective,
pages of a continuing body count mounting.
50,000 died from this ISH since this one started past the first page.

But you have to understand the level that it's impacted daily life for EVERYONE now.

The paranoia, the masking, the social distancing,
the impact on the world economy in every area.

Business after business now going under,
both a consequence of small businesses not able to
gain access to preventative funding because
large corporations got greedy and accessed loopholes
in a government law in 2020 which gave them the ability
to grab funding, that was never intended for them.

Some of them, when caught, (shamed and named) lookin like
shocked raccoons on page 5 of the news returned the money;
others kept it.

The financial logisitics of what took place, at the top, as millions of Americans were waiting week to week for unemployment checks to support themselves.

The short of a much longer story, is the Fed (The Federal Reserve) is printing empty money, backed up by nothing, except the belief that our currency can go on without end, without inflation catching up, but eventually it will.

The numerical consequences will eventually catch up but thats a quandary for the economists to handle and figure out. Not my circus, not my monetary monkies.

ANYWAYZ,
The bigger issue of it all isnt a possible financial crash, or American tensions increasing, though those things are likely across the board, we have issues that now cross through the roof until we can't stifle that if we dont get them under control.

American Markets, European Markets,
ALLLLLLLLLLL The markets are tied together.
All of us, in the same boat,
The rich, the poor, the dying middle class.

Titanic, did happen again.

The american debt is so high in the trillions, it's not even worth printing, as more empty, backless money is flying off printing presses.

When I crossed over from new years in 2019,
a repeat of the 1920's was NOT the 2020's
I wanted or prepared for.

Fuck.

Oh, I had a lot of criticism about my crass language
during the worst pandemic to strike during the past 100
years of time.

What's better, Sheila?

F bombs
or atomic bombs.

Better to say fuck - a few times - then
"Oh shit, we've got about 10 remaining seconds left to live."

This cannot be the first step into a new decade,
but here we fucking are.

Mother fucker.

??

6 million infections.
383,226+ dead bodies

100,000 dead americans from my side of the woods.

I expected a dazzling new step into a glorious new ten years,
a fresh start from the rocky road of the previous 20.

America - losing its final bit of Lady Liberty innocence - in September 11th,
Going off to war in 2003, a complete economic spiral
by 2008, hopelessness and joblessness that follow,
and degrees becoming harder to obtain
and even more worthless after all the work spent to get them.
Student Debt out the Wazoo, Mortgaged up to our titties.
Loans, Credit Cards, Deep in The Financial Hole
becomes the regular norm

Living paycheck to paycheck for the next twenty years.

Like LITERALLY living from one check to the next,
to keep jumping from one rope to the next.

But it ends up being just enough rope to hang ourselves, with.

You can't live paycheck to paycheck when you get furloughed,
fired, and lose your job from a virus that forces everyone
to shutter their windows and lock their doors.

For three months.

This novel is closure
while were closing caskets.

Truth is, we don't know how long it's gonna last for,

how many waves are gonna hit, and how many different mutations are going to make their way through the world's health channels, after a shamed and disowned world health organization is now on the risk of losing all major funding for their crimes against humanity.

Take that to a cards against humanity session.

5/20/2020

1:21:02 PM

From New Yorks 30,000 deaths, they've had 61,886 recover and 76,168 hospitalized
From New Jersey's 10,749 dead, they've had 23,657 recover and of the nearly 2 million infected inside the United States, 289,392 have recovered.

Russia has had a wild surge of infections,

totaling 308,705+ now infected with the viral outbreak.

spins the globe

Every nation, every area, every sovereignty
has now been infected and had to find the resources
to deal with this pathogen, pushing medical skill
to its highest possible level of workmanship and prowess,
against insane levels of exhaustion and (I'm sure) emotional
depletion.

Look at any land region on the map, and right now,
medical professionals working around the clock
on units with multiple patients suffering from C-19.

27,974 dead in France, 178,322 infected.
5,147 dead in Sao Paulo, Brazil, 65,995 infected.
7,183 dead in Iran, 126,949 infected.

27, 888 dead in Spain
35,785 UK dead
32,330 Italians gone

Please Pause,
Rewind,
Fast Forward,
Stop

Communistic Sickle-and-Hammer Time

27, 888 dead in Spain

Lets go back over a 100 years to the 1918 Spanish Flu which killed 20-100 million americans, with figures wildly differing from 20-100 because of a lack of concise medical records surviving/existing.

A much deadlier flu, with so many modern parallels, of healthy, robust people falling victim and succumbing to it, right and left.

Public gatherings stopped, business closed in the same way, masks were needed to slow the spread of a believed to be Avian born disease, that while called THE SPANISH FLU, isn't actually beleived to have originated in Spain.

More United States soldiers actually perished from IT instead of the first world War.

The second wave that spread was the deadliest, and that's where the greatest fear of relaxing restrictions currently is holding/hiding high anxiety.

A basis of historical reference is readily needed when we compare outbreaks between 1918 and now 2020.
First the name came from the fact that Spain was the only one reporting on the illness, while other countries were censoring news of the new virus because of them being currently engaged in War; they didn't want to freak out their troops with EVEN more bad news.

200,000 died in over ONE month from 1918,
Only 100,000 are dead in America in 2020

after several months,
but this isn't about which pathogen is greater,
this is about the importance OF social distancing
to slow those numbers down AND slow the spread.

Back then, they had no idea what was even going on, especially since the very first wave wasnt seen as all that dangerous; it was actually the secondary bit because of wartime movements of mass people that mutated it even further,
and created a true monster.

That same event is very possible to happen with COVID-19.

20-50 million DEAD, (two years)
compared to "only" 300,000+ (three months)

Current models and predictions are estimating a 700,000 total dead before the end of Summer
and then a return of more spikes in the fall,
with the new mutations emerging.

Deep Sigh

WEAR A MASK ... OR GO TO JAIL

Shows a group of people standing together in an old time photo of 1918.

It looks like the modern selfies today of everyone now
living behind forms of facial coverings.

Same exact mask style, with the loops around the ears.

History REALLY does repeat lmao.

Jeez. Covid Louise.

Spin the globe again

In area, in any country, in any town, city, and block,
you'll find people walking out, and working
behind face and surgical cloth masks to protect themselves,
At restaurants, Cashiers, in hotel lobbies, in grocery stores,
Any industry, place, or company, having its workers
breathing behind a thin strip of hopefully prevantative cloth.

What is the bigger lesson of all these smaller learning
lessons?

To not jimmy around with dangerous pathogens?
To not create chimeric, mult9i-strain viral monsters?
To not place the blame on a wetmarket?
To not lie about the spread and cover it up?

knocks globe off the table

Hell if know what the actual lesson is, at this point,
I'd just like to get through this dumb thing.

There are multi-level points of the "lesson," but
all of this could have been avoided or at least greatly

minimized.

The silence of the outbreak, the secret testing from one country looking for different cures and one global health organization covering
for each other, hastened and created something... that had it have been addressed properly had literallt anyone - BEEN ALLOWED - to speak up and not reprimanded.

EYEROLL

I don't know how else to impart the severity of this KIND of stupidity.

It makes you wonder how close were always on the edge of some major, perilous collapse; moments away from some cataclysmic event from sheer dumb people,
but kept going by sheer dumb luck.

I don't think I wanna know the answer.

Anyway, Times Five, Now that it's (Miss Covid-19) is out and about, the United States Armed forces has declared
anyone that contracts COVID cannot enlist or serve, ever,
in the armed forces, because of the unknown total-body damage and inflammation it does to the lungs, hearts and other organs.

The bigger issue, while a vaccine is in the centrifugal, biopharmaceutical works,
is not knowing the scope of damage that it performs upon the body or the long-term consequences of what it can or cannot

do, after we get into the nitty-gritty of what goes on on the cellular, pathological, viralogical, immunological.... All the logical pathways of pure illogic insanity.

SEVERE ACUTE RESPIRATORY SYNDROME

COUGH COUGH

2003 for SARS 1

2012 for MERS, Middle Eastern Resp. Syndrome

2020 for SARS 2 COV

GLOWBULL EKANOMICK KAH-TAS-TROPHY

US + 22,464 new infections in one night
Worldwide + 110,000 confirmed infections in one night

lmfa....o

This is so fucked up

"A small cluster of cases return in Wuhan, The city where it all began."

EYE YAI YAI

Jesus Mary Corona Christ

IDEK man...
The rest of this year and the next will be spent funneling cash into a vaccine, herd immunity will have to come into

place, but until then, it's gonna be.... not business as usual.... and the summer of cloth surgical #N95masks.

As people get overconfident of their safety
and start dropping like flies

In cycles of respiratory sickness,

HASHTAG #PESTILENCE

I just wanna say some final words on Bill Gates and his "Event 201" Pandemic Preperation "Scenario" that was run in OCTOBER 2019.

From the Center of Health Security.Org

Please just read this shit

Remember, this was a hypothetical "SITUATION" - created on world stage - using a ZOONOTIC CORONAVIRUS TRANSMITTED FROM BATS

MONTHS BEFORE THE CURRENT CORONA VIRUS COMES OUT.

...... these are all their OWN words. Not Mine. This is their very own description.

Not a word has been changed.

READ IT:

Reads with a microphone from their very own conference paper they used

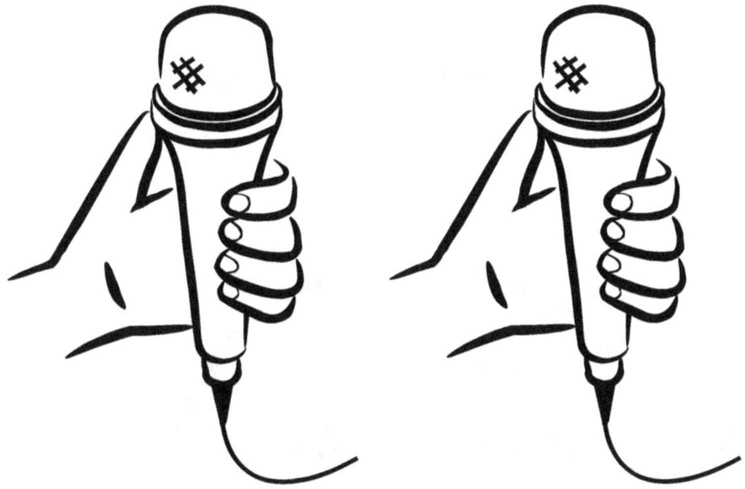

AHEM …. HERE WE GO.

"Event 201 simulates an outbreak of a novel zoonotic coronavirus transmitted from bats to pigs to people that eventually becomes efficiently transmissible from person to person, leading to a severe pandemic. The pathogen and the disease it causes are modeled largely on SARS, but it is more transmissible in the community setting by people with mild symptoms.

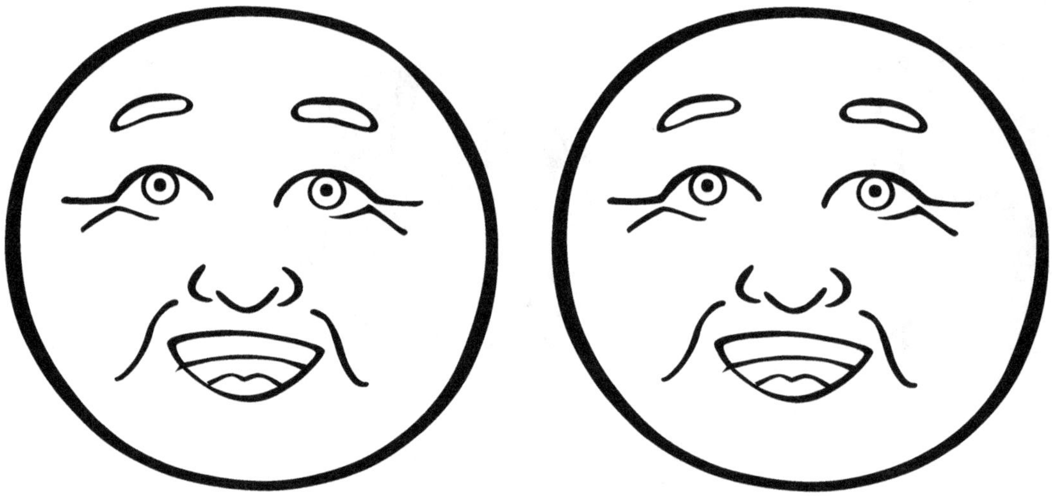

The disease starts in pig farms in Brazil, quietly and slowly at first, but then it starts to spread more rapidly in healthcare settings. When it starts to spread efficiently from person to person in the low-income, densely packed neighborhoods of some of the megacities in South America, the epidemic **explodes**. It is first exported by air travel to Portugal, the United States, and China and then to many other countries. Although at first some countries are able to control it, it continues to spread and be reintroduced, and eventually no country can maintain control.

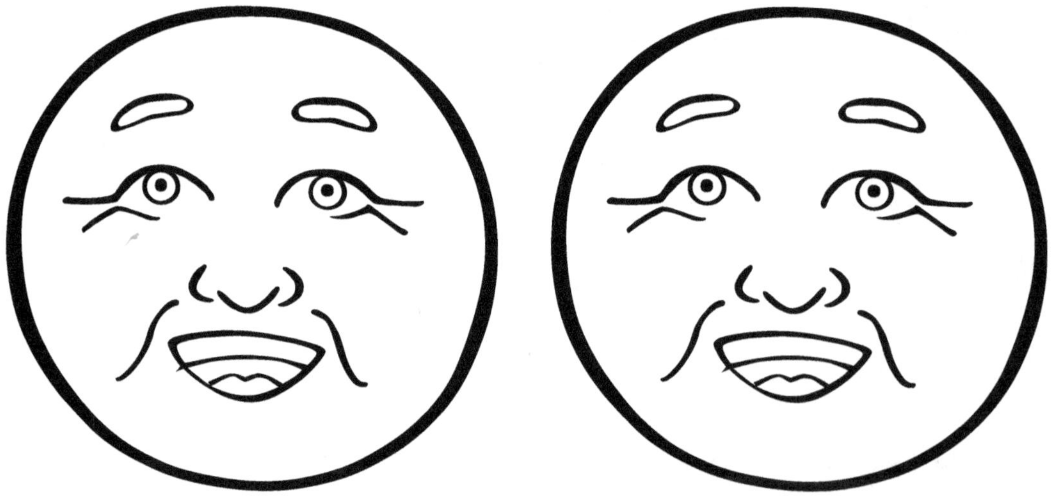

There is no possibility of a vaccine being available in the first year. There is a fictional antiviral drug that can help the sick but not significantly limit spread of the disease. (Still all their OWN words)

Since the whole human population is susceptible, during the initial months of the pandemic, the cumulative number of cases increases exponentially, doubling every week. And as the cases and deaths accumulate, the economic and societal **consequences become increasingly severe.**

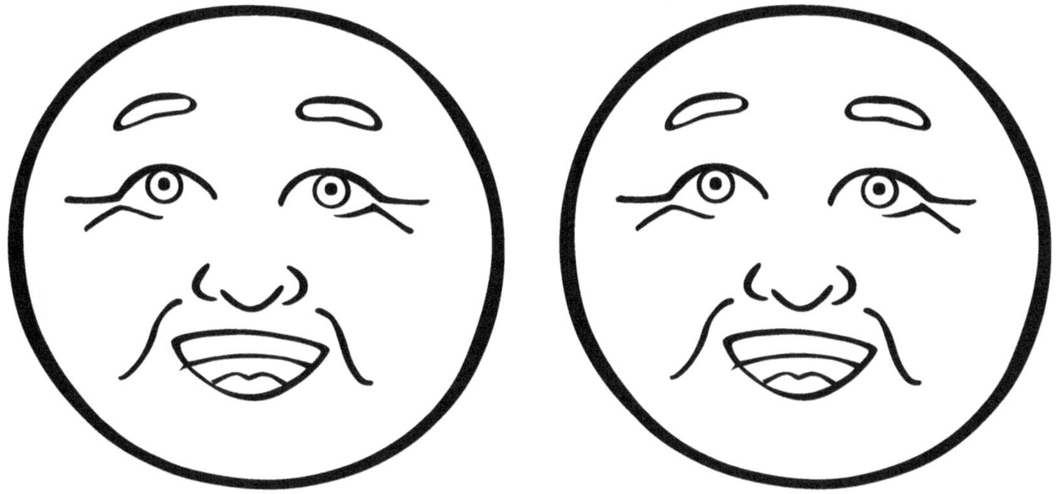

The scenario ends at the 18-month point, with 65 million deaths. The pandemic is beginning to slow due to the decreasing number of susceptible people. The pandemic will continue at some rate until there is an effective vaccine or until 80-90 % of the global population has been exposed. From that point on, it is likely to be an endemic childhood disease."

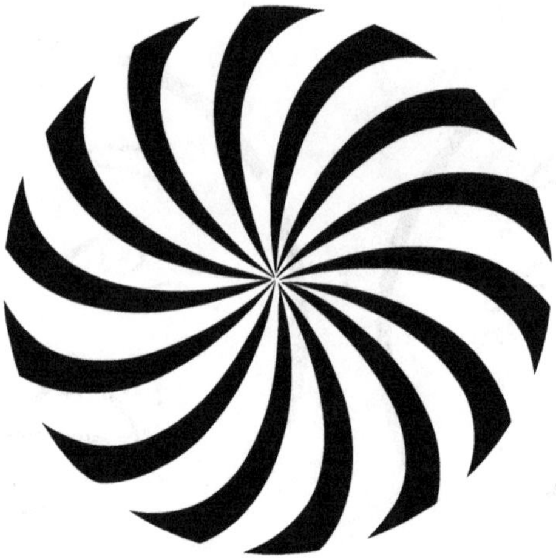

X-RAY
VISION

....

....

....

Yo.

They modeled a "fictional" CORONA VIRUS

two months before a REAL one comes out.

That wording.

That entire excerpt.

I can't stand it.

I can't stand a single bit of it.

It's too Coicdental. Im sorry.

The timing, the wording, the specific use of a Zoonotic spread.

I hate this whole thing.

It smells like shit.

Domina Petric acquired a copy of EVENT 201's manuscript, and I want you to look at THIS.

The Event models a spread of a brand new ZOONOTIC Coronavirus
spread from bats to PEOPLE that creates an outbreak from person to person.
Eventually leading to a severe PANDEMIC.

The pathogen and the the "fake" disease it causes
were modeled largely on SARS

Among the selected "game players" at this table was the professor George Fu Gao,
who is director of the Chinese Center for
Disease Control and Prevention since
2017. George FU specializes specifically in research
on influenza interspecies
transmission (host jump).

--Domina Petric

END QUOTE.

They got these people listed as PLAYERS, like some messed up Super Smash Bros. LINEUP .... IM DECEASED

IN AN URN.

....

It's literally the SCRIPT of this whole thing.

Previous SARS virus, backbone, becomes structure of SARS2 (ALIAS AKA CORONA VIRUS; COVID-19)

A ZOONOTIC CORONA VIRUS, specifically...

NEW PANDEMIC

Whole human population is in danger to this "fictional" virus...

No Cure or Vaccine Ready....

Director of the Chinese CDC, who specializes in interspecies transmissibility....

From the Actual Wuhan Chinese institute of virology...

YET THIS IS SOMEHOW A SIMULATION??

LESS THAN TWO MOTHA FU...CKIN MONTHS

BEFORE THIS SHIT HAPPENS??????????????????????

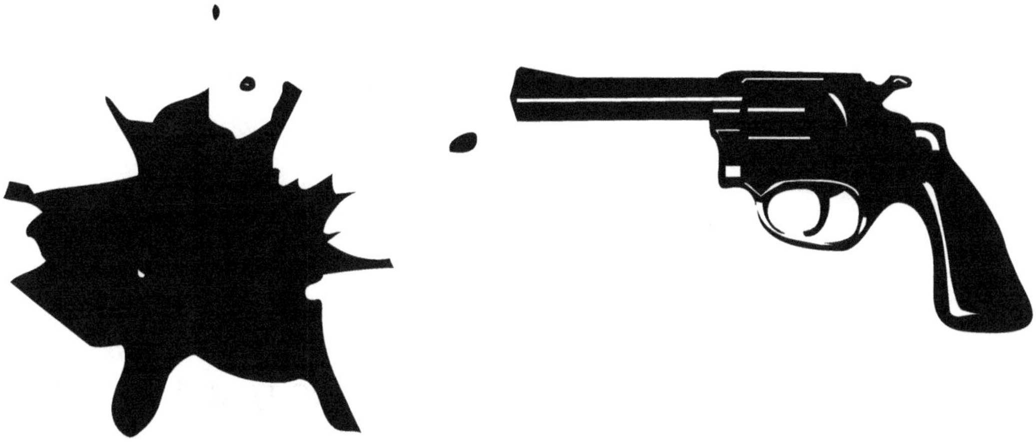

This just gets worse, and worse, and worse, and WORSE

No charges, no nothing has been filed on these people

Nothing. They're in the media, smiling.

Man, oh fuckin MAN............

You can't make this shit up.

Listen to the Highlight Reel of it.

NOVEMBER 4th, 2019

This is from the CENTER OF HEALTH SECURITY...

"Infected people get a respiratory illness
with symptoms ranging from flu like, to severe Pneumonia.
The sickest will require intensive care and many

will die."

THIS IS FROM BILL GATES "SIMULATION" VIDEO

FROM THE WEBSITE

"The next severe pandemic will not only cause great illness and loss of life but could also trigger major cascading economic and societal consequences that could contribute greatly to global impact and suffering."

I'm going to level a

high
charge.

But this.

Is terrorism.

When/where

Friday, October 18, 2019
8:45 a.m. – 12:30 p.m.
The Pierre hotel
New York, NY
Audience

An invitation-only audience of nearly 130 people attended the exercise.

They really sat in a meeting and discussed a new, novel Corona Virus and what it was going to do as a "game." Like it was some kind of speculative entertainment

Microbial Gladitorial Sport.

OH MY FUCKIN GOD.

ALMIGHTY.

They played around with the idea of 65 million PEOPLE dead.

SICK. MOTHER. FUCKERS.

The Real New Corona Virus goes live in December, after this "Fictional" invitation only meeting.

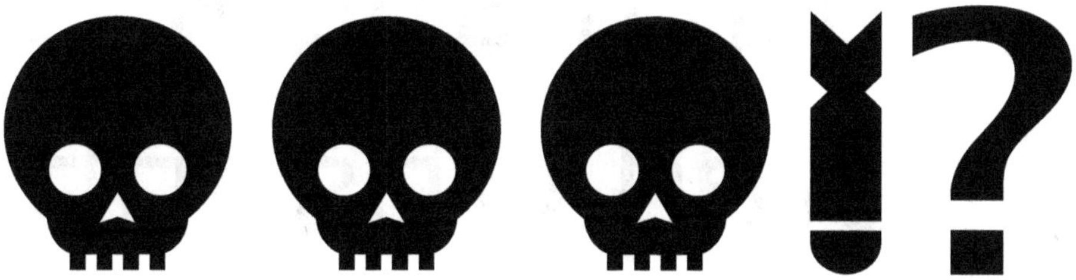

Modeled largely on SARS

flashback

"We built a chimeric virus encoding a novel, zoonotic Cov Spike protein, in the context of the SARS adapted backbone -- to cause disease from a hybrid virus independently of other necessary adaptive mutations in its natural backbone."

-Published November 9th, TWENTY FIFTEEN (2015)

Menachery, V., Yount, B., Debbink, K. et al. A SARS-like cluster of circulating bat coronaviruses shows potential for human emergence. Nat Med 21, 1508-1513 (2015)

Jesus, Mary and a Flu Infected Joseph.

2015, you have the recipe. THE UNDENIABLE SCIENCE NOTES TO DO THIS.
2016, the warnings it could/might/WILL happen
2017, the articles discussing it in third person
FAUCI going in front of a camera and saying the president will get to deal
with a surprise "PANDEMIC."
2018-2019, a round table of rich scumbags to "simulate" a new zoonotic, corona virus
but it's all just "pretend" and for "fun."

2020 - a real corona virus then "escapes" from a lab with a zoonotic protein

spike
from BATS.

STARES IN DISBELIEF

#Policy and public health in microbiology
#SARS virus
#Translational research
#Viral infection

HASHTAG #YA GOTTA BE FUCKIN KIDDING ME.

Let's go back to the "SIMU-FUCKING-LATION."

"There is no possibility of a vaccine being available in the first year. There is a fictional antiviral drug that can help the sick but not significantly limit spread of the disease.

Since the whole human population is susceptible, during the initial months of the pandemic, the cumulative number of cases increases exponentially, doubling every week."

In REAL LIFE, outside of the fucked up Matrix they've now created,
It's correct, even if everything goes perfectly, We wont have an FDA approved
Vaccine for 8-12 months.

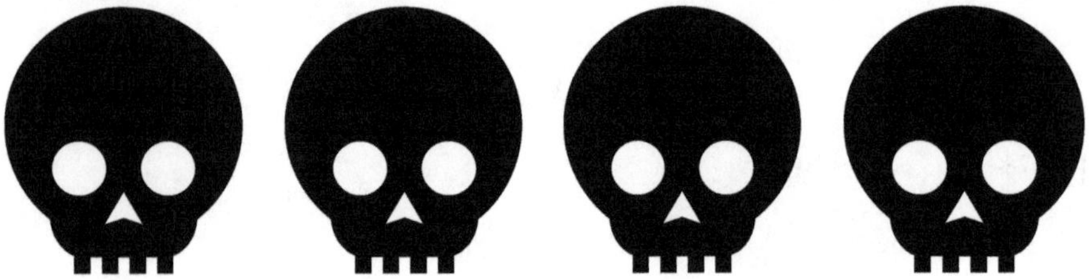

Then to say that the cumulative number doubles and increases
isn't just foretelling of a possible outbreak,
it's exactly what happened

Not because of a "TOLD YOU SO" moment
but because this moment was Probably Planned.

These Doctors, This Planned Pandemic, This
SIMULATION,
THIS EVENT,

The shadiness, the suspect timing, the impossible coincidence of a
ZOONOTIC CORONA virus, with a protein spike, that was engineered
in 2015, suddenly "escaping" and wreaking havoc......

I have never once believed in a single, conspiracy out there....

But No way.

No way, do all these dots MAGICALLY connect,
by absolute "chance."

These people are all in league with each other.

Watch the world burn a bit, stand behind the chemical companies
reading a pharma cure, and profit like no other, while acting concerned.

This is pure, evil.

Oh, China is Bad,

But this is BAD BAD BAD BAD BAD BAD

I dont think I wanna know anymore,
I dont think I care to find out how much deeper this goes down

How much more malicious it gets.

The evilness that hides behind the human smile.

The syringe of shadiness waiting in the shadows.

The doctors, these virologists, these immunologists have the charge of studying disease to PREVENT IT

Not TO CAUSE IT.

This is so so so so so awful.

WHAT

THE

F.U...C.K

WHAT
THE
FUCK.

I just dont think you go set down in a hotel with a select number of top officials, plan an imaginary pandemic that mirrors everything currently happening and then turn around and laugh it off as it being "all fun and games."

I think it's like a Tornado chaser,
they get so wildly excited about the "NEXT BIG STORM" coming,
that they titillate on edge, to be in the moment.

I think this is exciting, in the same way, but more perversely and with higher stakes for these virologists,
that something going this VIRAL,
now isn't outside the realm of possibility of them, if not all of them,
Knowing what was coming down the pipeline.

I think its sick,
You have something making people sick, killing them,
damaging their bodies,
damaging an entire world economy...
and its even sicker,
that this whole thing has a previously made script.

With the very virus, KAH-RONA, very same spread mechanism.

It's unbelievable that people could or WOULD do something like this.

At first, it's angry at a nation that lied and experimented with this pathogen,
destroyed samples, covered up, ran the world health organization and its leader
inside its backpocket, allowed it to spread all over China and to the US, the world, Italy, all these places...

But now, it's like.... You have a panel of esteemed scientists poised for this moment.

It's pure poison. Waiting and Hoping - And very probably - helping cause this whole fucking thing.

All it would take, is sending these samples to the Wuhan Lab, having them open it, without them even knowing what it was.... and BAM.

There are a million ways for these simulation architects to have aided in this.

Im in disbelief at how messy and messed up this has gotten.

It feels like a Wargame.

"We want to have a centalized source of information... A world body that could have garned the respect of everyone and the

W.H.O. is that."

This was said six weeks before it actually goes "off."

And the World Health Organization is NOT that body.

Pause
\
Pause this whole god damn thing, HEAUX
Pause it JUST like you would in a "simulation."

This is the real thing. The Real Deal.
Real people are dead from it.

I think......... and this is stepping away from the whole thing with the vantage point of perspective

I think, it makes perfect sense why Trump was placed into power.

The country is so polarized of right + left, nobodies listening, people are busy arguing and pointing fingers, taking shots at each other, the president, the country...

In all THAT chaos and confusion.

It's a perfect, opportunistic storm.

If you were gonna do some really messed up, shady, stuff..
NOW is the time

You maneuver a figure into power, who causes extreme reactions.
And the figure himself, doesnt hold the real power,
He's an political twitter puppet
for people behind the scenes more sinister.

I don't think Trump even realizes the kinds of backstabbing people
that are pulling the strings.

Trump has never been a threat. He's never been mildly offensive to me.
He's just another All American Male.
People dont wanna hear it, but its the truth.

What has "shocked" everyone else, isn't really shocking.

What IS shocking, however, is now is the perfect time to render America,
and by extension, the connected global economy a series of

devastating hits.

Granted, the simulation models 65 million dead, and god help us if the second wave mutates out to those kind of insane numbers, and while I think this whole thing was now planned, I dont think it will go according to plan.

But Im watching Americans fight each other and say bitchy comments
about each other... Just thinking.... Its not trump, its not the democrats,
its not the republicans... though everybody is guilty and nobody is innocent here...

Its whoever is behind all these groups and people that is the REAL threat.

An entire country is trying to reopen, while yelling at each other....

It's just the perfect time to take advantage of the anger, and turn people against each other even more.

Im not even implying the existence of some shadowy organization lmao

Were not talking about the "illuminati" or something stupid, but I do believe
theres way more going on then just this.

Do we say its nefarious globalists wanting to create a centralized world, with a centralized worldview after killing and reaping a massive toll of the inhabitants?

I dont know and I think to speak on this becomes too quickly speculative and wildly all-over-the-place, but what I will say is, I dont think theres something good behind all this.

I think it may be a level and degree of subtle corruption that goes all the way down

I dont what the agenda is, I dont what kind of hidden agenda could be taking place. You have lots of powerful egos constantly clashing with each other.

Im just a member of the GP (GENERAL PUBLIC) in the MIDWEST... of all places

I just know how to do the proper digging and dig correctly in ways most dont.
I dont mean that arrogantly, but it requires a certain kind of investigative skillset and keen eye to spot the lies and they come out.

Im a human lie detector, which makes this work flow in the way it does.

I dont think Ill ever get over buying my calender for 2020 and it being titled
"Hidden Agenda."

between THAT and event 201, and now the world suffering in this moment of chaos....

I dont think I'll get over how insanely communal and strange this whole thing has been.

I really feel like, at any moment, that I will *wake* up.

It feels so dystopian, even when I was writing the previous book "KONG FLU PANDA" #KFP, it was like I was writing a made-up tale about a global event.

It's too surreal to process and now looking at these data sets that strongly and highly suggest that this was a manufactured event, with a manufactured viral pathogen, that goes back five years, from a prexisting SARS spread, 18 years ago... This doesnt seem real.

Im reporting the situation - as it emerges - but I dont know what I really think about it.

It's too BIG to wrap my mind around that people could do something like this,
out of boredom.

Why would you destabilize peoples live like this and try close business and kick the crap out of peoples livelihoods?

And then try and kill them all?
I mean you think a holocaust is BAD? Thats 8 million.
They were modeling (hoping) for 65 million
That's eight separate holocausts.

I can't fathom something like this.

It literally feels like some wild conspiracy post you stumble online,
with all these connecting points that become TOO much,
that by the end of it, you go, ".... Yeah... right..."

But for this to BE what it is..

I mean....

I just cant lmao

Here is the true catch-22 of it all.

Nobody is going to believe any of this.
If I heard someone say all this, I'd be like "Pfft, OKAYYY, whatever you say."

It's done SO boldly in BROAD daylight, there's no way it seems plausible.

It connects SO well, it seems too perfect.

I feel like a reporter asking the camera men "if they're getting all this"
AS it's happening.

I think people were hoping for a crash. A Cascade of events that would wipe the slate clean.

Nations targeting Nations.

Fingers pointing to one country

and China, is still guilty,

but you have intentions that are like a global guillotine now.

We could all lose our heads,
if we dont keep them on tight right now.

Whats the end goal of all this? Tabletop death simulation?

Whats the end game?

Catastrophic world War? Collapse by Nuclear Immolation?

I dont care to speculate about what ifs, but I do know this was a Global Domino event,
and not all of the pieces fell correctly, but whoever pushed the first piece,
was hoping for something
WAYYYYYYYYYYYYYYYYYYYYY Worse.

And it very well could have occured.

People were playing with fate, here.

Playing WITH FIRE 

Conclusion: A manufactured virus emerges from a region, the region denies all responsibility, the virus spreads and infects millions, kills over a quarter of a million in the first wave, could mutate into worse strands and take out untold numbers and strongly harming population. A panel of experts planned a specific simulation with the same exact virus as a tabletop game with disease control experts 2 months before a real life event happens, lies everywhere, in every direction. Incompetence, Chaos, Confusion, Unrest, Anger, Ineptitude, Falsification, Geopolitical Distrust, Dots that Connect themselves, and a fatal flu virus taking bodybags with it, will continue to hurt people and the pot of coins we exist on for an unknown duration. Social Media isn't adding clarity to the narrative but actually confusing things even more.
It seems like this was the intended aim.

LEMME RESAY IT TWICE.

A novel virus, w/ shady origins that sweeps away 350,000 dead in a few months, an acting president that polarizes and

nobody takes seriously, creating a void of American leadership, lies in every direction, chaos, confusion, unrest, anger, falsification, dots that connect themselves, finger pointing, an economy laying on the ground in shock and trying to stabilize and NOW, race relations and frustrations popping off from both sides, and boiling over with each other.
WHAT a convenient time to pit people against each other and make them fight, rant and yell online with escalating tensions, while whatever is happening behind the scenes goes unnoticed. There are too many complicated pieces in motion and it doesn't look good from any angle. While Im watching everyone fight, I get the eery feeling that all of these dominos were pushed - purposely - while the real trouble is moving, unnoticed.

The prelude to War was attempted.

What's really worrying.
I mean really scary.

I have a feeling this was just the trial version.
This feels like a test to see how it would play out,
before launching the real thing

They got their results in the simulation and now in real time.

They know how to strike better, how to better optimize a new virus,
how to write the coding sequence for something even deadlier.

Theyve seen how governments respond,

the ineffectiveness, the mass panic, the breakdown of financial markets

They got the sneak peek it feels like they wanted.

After a cataclysmic loss of trust,

I worry worse may come.

I think that behind every lab coat, of a concerned doctor archetype,
is a ill intentioned wolf. Hiding.

The media is a dumb echo chamber, the people are mostly .... mediocre.
Theres nothing really sinister about either.

It is what it is.

But I fear there is some higher level of social "country club" with exclusive access for its members behind this that truly does wish ill on the world.

You know its the narrative of "The democrats are the enemy" or "The republicans are the enemy" or "The media is the real enemy."

Yall.. I hate to be an ass, but none of you are really that smart or deadly.

You're each others and your own worst enemy,
but its like a schoolyard of kids all throwing rocks at each other.

I worry behind the metal fence, there are adults watching the playground with some cruel intentions.

And trying to convince anyone, nobody is going to listen, there are political rocks being hurled everywhere.

Fighting each other, is what they - the ever elusive, vague, THEY - want.

It feels like a social experiment, and now mixed with a deadly lab experiment.

I think, if I live through this, I'll watch the same story of Democrats vs Repubs, play out, again + again, in infinite forms, but I think, I'll never get past this sense of paranoia of watching eyes beyond those two groups thats watching from the periphery window down on all of us.

its that feeling, in public, when you can just FEEL someone looking at you,
and you turn, and lock eyes with them.

It's something intuitive, and less logical.

To base a conclusion on that kind of a premise, is not how I wanna end things,
But I just have this apprehension from all this, that its just the

tip of the iceburg.

Im gonna watch Americans tare down each other, and fight,
I'm not gonna step into the fray.... because my time will be
spent walking around the perimeter, looking for the weak
spots in the fence, keeping us all in here.

I think it's the best I can do.

If its not Clinton, Its Bush, If its not Bush its Obama, if its Not
Obama, its Trump. And then whoever comes up to the game of
American thrones, next.

On and on this wheel goes,
But whatever is turning it - is where the real story of this
goes.

The succession of power,
and the sins that happen during each turn...

Im starting to think America isnt a dream, but a nightmare.

Keep them working, keep them busy,
Keep the people divided, keep them hating each other,
keep them at odds over issues,
Keep them standing at points of inequality....

Keep the whole entire show going.

Lab Experiment gone Wrong,
Social Landscape experiment gone wrong.

Lemme be the most honest with you possible.
And its gonna be offensive, but being really honest usually is.

I love this country. I really, really do.
For all its juxtaposition, madness, insanity in that red, white and blue.
For of all of its historical nonsense.

I love it. I love freedom, so I love America.

HOW-FLIPPIN-EVER
I dont love the inability to provide for yourself,
I dont love the ratrace that goes nowhere,
I dont love the impossible cost of living.

But Ill always love the basis of what my homeland has given me.
My voice can echo, because I have the freedom to say THESE things.

But... with how its going... if I had enough money, Id drain my accounts
and get out of here.

Id get citizenship elsewhere and stay until the Wild, Wild West
returns to a more psychologically balanced and less toxic, depressing place.

You have mass shootings everyday of the month,
Religious factors, Insanity of right vs left, in a Player Vs Player type match,
Increasing division, increasing unrest, and that was before a

global pandemic
smacked us.

You have a two hour hospital visit that charges 65,000 dollars for a basic procedure, causing medical bankruptcy around the table.

It's just all gotten... to be .... too much and also not enough.

I feel like Im in the Garden of the New Rome.

The CONSTANT DRAMA of this place and bottleneck of wealth....

I dont feel connected to the political fighting, I registered as an Independent
at age 18, I still feel that same exact way.
I dont feel connected to the Gay World, Let alone the straight world.

Its just so much nonsense noise.

Its just not fulfilling anymore.

To try and create a better direction and stick your hand in the social hornets nest, its not gonna play out with some revolutionary new way.

Where we storm the capitals and demand independence or something...
Lmao

shrug

People wont listen
but Americans REALLY wont listen lmao

sits back at desk and looks at the globe

I miss strong, effective leadership, I miss SOME sense of unity,
I miss a lot of the things that were around, even in a hodgepodge
of different ideas that seem to be gone these days.

I feel like we've just changed, and not in a good way.

blows bubbles with political theory books behind me

IDK anymore lmao

bubble drops down on Karl Marx

It is what it is people, sugar were going down swinging.

lets rainbow tinted translucent bubbles continue to pop around the room

lights a cig and sighs

stares out through the garden window

Sees the Chinese Geraniums in the wind

eyebrow twitches

THE END

Deleted Scene

Fire roars in a warm study lounge

The starting astrological age of Aquarius, the last air sign,
has a global airway related illness that stops the ability to breathe,
as protestors for a murdered black man scream at police in Minnesota
"WE CAN'T BREATHE."
Aquarius deals with the collective and its relationship to the individual.

Funny thing, life is sometimes.

The virus that infects the human airway paths,
The masks stopping citizens from being able to get full air,
The police holding people down who suffocate on the ground

The 371, 987 dead whose lungs shutdown and died of asphyxiation
from a manmade virus.

lights a fat cigar

breathes out

It all just takes my breath away

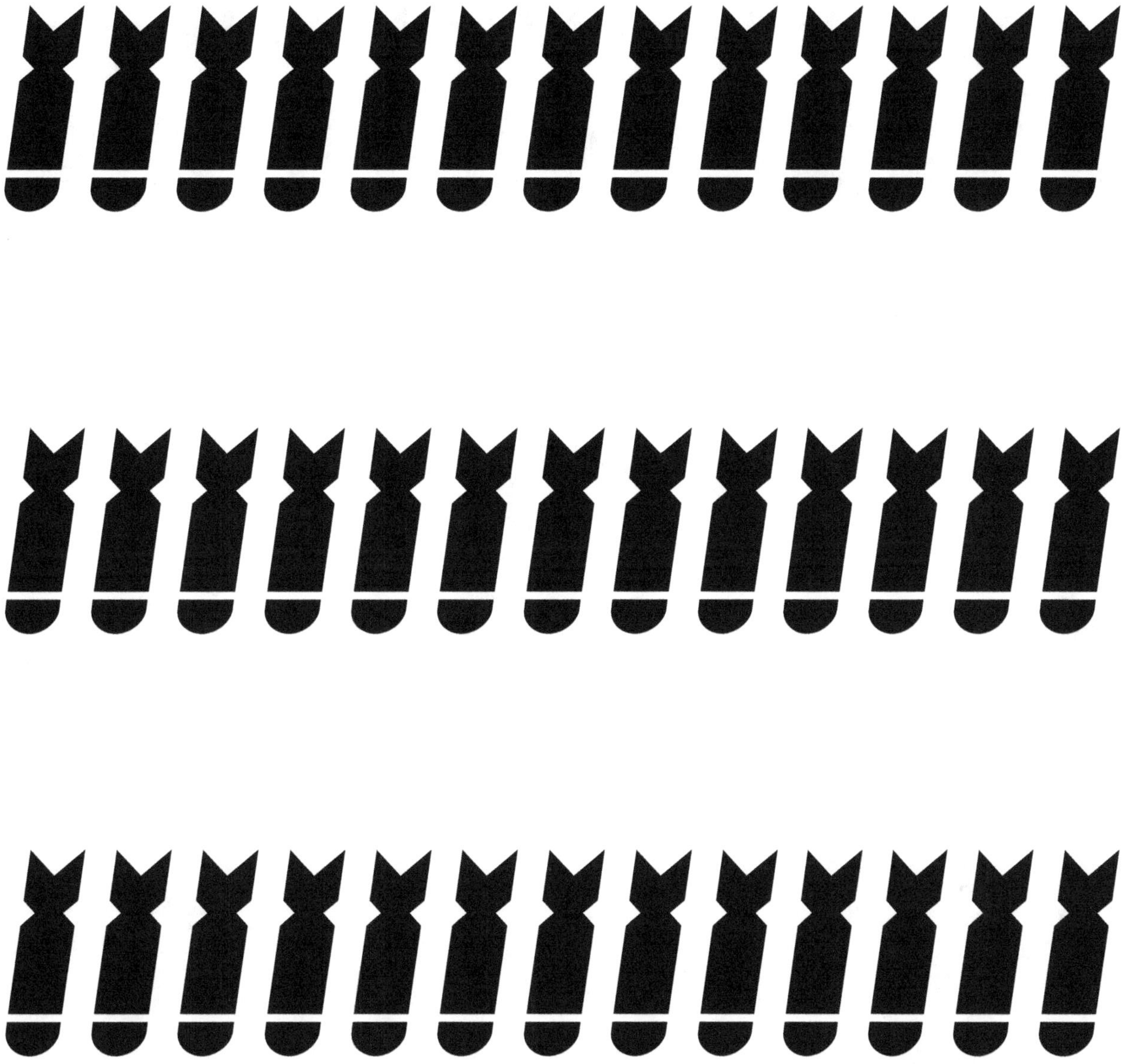

Back in Minneapolis, where Black men are killed by police,
and where an infection is still spreading,silently,
As people riot outside, loudly,
A hospital scene unfolds

PATIENT

is CODING

God Damnit, The infection has gone too far inside his

lungs,

...we're losing him.
Multiple Organ Failure,
Liver showing unnatural enzyme
numbers
Respirator is inflaming his
breathing pathways,
Heart rate is currently stuttering

DO SOMETHING!

We're trying, okay, but we can't get
his lungs to open up for us,
There's too much fluid built up
inside
He's Drowning right on dry land

Doctor, you're too emotional
and not thinking clearly
Step away from the patient,

Please, go outside now and remove your mask

Doctor Flings Gloves off and walks out

FLATLINE
END OF THE LINE

ECMO
Extracorporeal
Membrane Oxygenation
Frontline Failure
Lymphocyte count deteriorated

COVID

19

FATALI TY

+1 to kill count

−1 to life on earth

I whispered to the angel beside me
who was the Angel of Death
He said I'll take Ü somewhere
beautiful
I muttered
in my last breath...
Just take me away from here

BegiN
OperatioN
DepopulatioN

VIRAL KONG

FLU

SOCIAL

KUNG FU

One was created and opened on society in ignorance in China

The other, is kept going by social + racial ignorance across the globe

www.ingramcontent.com/pod-product-compliance
Lightning Source LLC
Chambersburg PA
CBHW081348040426
42450CB00015B/3355
* 9 7 8 0 5 7 8 7 0 6 8 0 1 *